HOW TO SURVIVE ALMOST ANYTHING

by **Brooks Whitney**

SCHOLASTIC INC.

New York   Toronto   London   Auckland   Sydney

Mexico City   New Delhi   Hong Kong   Buenos Aires

The recommendations and advice included in this book are based
on research and expert information. The publisher and author have made
every effort to ensure that the information presented is complete and accurate.
This book is not intended to replace professional advice, which you should seek
in case of an emergency. In the event of a real emergency, readers should consult
their parents, teachers, or other professionals and experts such as doctors, police,
and poison control. The publisher, author, and illustrator disclaim any liability for
any injury that may result from the use of the information in this book.

ISBN: 0-439-57900-7

Design: Julie Mullarkey Gnoy
Illustrations: Kelly Kennedy

Copyright © 2004 by Scholastic Inc.

All rights reserved. Published by Scholastic Inc.

SCHOLASTIC, HOW TO SURVIVE ANYTHING, and associated logos are
trademarks and/or registered trademarks of Scholastic Inc.

12 11 10 9 8 7 6 5 4   4 5 6 7 8 9/0

Printed in the U.S.A.

First Scholastic printing, January 2004

CONTENTS

There are going to be times when you find yourself in an **unexpected situation**. It might be something that's frightening, or challenging, or annoying, or embarrassing, or just plain hard. This **survival handbook** is especially for you to help you during times like those. It's your answer-filled guide to solving all sorts of life's big—and not so big—challenges.

Go ahead—take a look. From bee stings to bullies, *How to Survive Almost Anything* is packed with ideas for **surviving** all sorts of sticky situations! You'll find solutions to **tricky stuff**, like what to do when a **friend asks you to steal** or what to do if you're **caught lying**. You'll get tips for all kinds of **icky stuff**, from getting **gum off** the bottom of **your shoe** to what to do if you **throw up at school**. You'll learn how to use your **watch as a compass**, make a **first-aid kit**, calculate how far away **lightning** is, **how to evacuate a building** in an emergency, and what to do when there's a **fire**! You'll get advice about **embarrassing moments** like when you **drop your lunch tray** in front of the whole cafeteria, and **scary moments** like what happens if you find yourself on **thin ice**. You'll also get to know how to deal with **school stuff**, **siblings, strangers, storms**—and lots more!

You'll find that there's a way to survive *almost anything*— and that you can do it! Plus there are cool **projects** like how to make a sling and how to map out a fire-escape route, and special **quizzes** so you can **test your survival knowledge** for different situations. At the end of the book, you'll even get to quiz yourself to see how much you've improved your survival skills. But most important, you'll learn strategies that can be used to help **solve almost any problem**, not just the ones in this book. Knowing how to go about solving a problem is the first step to solving it!

Along with this survival guide, this month's survival gadgets include:

 • **Survival Bag** with eight pockets for stashing your survival gear

 • **Glow-in-the-dark Whistle** to call for help

 • Secret **Lighted Cash Stash Keychain** for keeping emergency money safe and hidden

 • **Flashlight** for power outages and other emergencies

Whenever you see these gadget pictures throughout the book, it means that you can use your survival tools to help you survive the situation!

You can read this guide **cover to cover**, or dip into any section you like. If you've got a particular situation you want help with right now, flip to that section and start there. If your specific issue isn't in this book, find a similar situation and see if that strategy can help you. With this guide, your gadgets, and your common sense, you can feel **confident** in your ability **to survive just about anything**!

POP QUIZ

What's Your Survivor Know-How?

Before you start, find out just how much you already know! How good are your survival instincts? Take this quiz, then check your score.

1. You're hiking through the woods, when it begins to **thunder** and **lightning**. You immediately seek shelter under the tallest tree you can find.
   - **a.** That's me
   - **b.** I might do that
   - **c.** I'd never do that

2. You're playing ball in the park when a **ferocious dog** charges at you. You start running for the safety of the public bathrooms in the distance.
   - **a.** That's me
   - **b.** I might do that
   - **c.** I'd never do that

3. It's a snowy day and you and a friend are enjoying the outdoors. You come to a **frozen pond** in the middle of the woods. You jump right onto the ice without a second thought.
   - **a.** That's me
   - **b.** I might do that
   - **c.** I'd never do that

4. You're on vacation and you get separated from your parents in the city you're visiting. A **nice stranger** offers to drive you back to your hotel. You happily accept the ride.
   - **a.** That's me
   - **b.** I might do that
   - **c.** I'd never do that

5. You answer the **phone** and it's a person taking a survey. If you answer their questions, you could win a trip. They ask for your name, age, and address, which you spout off immediately. Anything to win that trip!
   - **a.** That's me
   - **b.** I might do that
   - **c.** I'd never do that

6. You live on the tenth floor of an apartment building and the **fire** alarm goes off. You run into the hallway and look for the quickest exit. You choose the elevator because it's much faster than taking the stairs.
   - **a.** That's me
   - **b.** I might do that
   - **c.** I'd never do that

7. You come home after school to an empty house and realize that you **left your key** on the kitchen table this morning. You go around back and try to crawl up the rain gutter to a second-story window.

  a. That's me
  b. I might do that
  c. I'd never do that

8. It's your third week at Camp Fun in the Sun and you know you'll be out on the water all day. But since the skies are cloudy, you don't bring along any **sunscreen** because you don't think you'll need it.

  a. That's me
  b. I might do that
  c. I'd never do that

9. You're about to give a three-minute speech to your class about your favorite book, but the minute you get in front of everyone, you can't even **remember** the title! You run out of the room and spend the rest of the day hiding in the bathroom.

  a. That's me
  b. I might do that
  c. I'd never do that

10. You're alone at home and the **power goes out.** You know you have an extra flashlight lying around somewhere, but you're not sure where it is.

  a. That's me
  b. That might be me
  c. That would never be me

Check Your Survival Skills

Give yourself **two points** for every **c** that you circled. Give yourself **one point** for every **b**. Give yourself **zero points** for every **a**.

Super Survivor *(15-20 points)*
Great problem solving! Your common sense and smart thinking will get you out of all sorts of sticky situations. You know to take time to think things through before you act. Keep using your head!

Satisfactory Survivor *(8-14 points)*
There's room for improvement. But not to worry: That's what this book is for! If you're not absolutely sure what to do, remember to stay calm and think through all your options *before* making a decision.

SOS: Save Our Survivor! *(0-7 points)*
Your hasty decisions make matters worse! Take a deep breath and evaluate your situation. If you think before you act, you're sure to come up with a smart—and safe—solution. And here's a newsflash: You're sure to do better on this quiz (so come back to it) once you read this book!

The Great Outdoors

From swimming and sailing to hiking and ice-skating, being outdoors is a real pleasure. But sometimes an activity can become a problem when you least expect it. Whether it's a sudden cramp in your leg while swimming, or a thunderstorm during a hike, these what-to-do tips will come in handy.

HOW TO SURVIVE NATURE

CAUGHT IN A THUNDERSTORM

What do you do if you're caught outside when a thunderstorm comes rolling in?

✔ **Be prepared.** Look for darkening skies, lightning, and increased wind, and listen for thunder. If you hear thunder, you're close enough to the storm to be struck by lightning. Go find shelter. The safest place is inside a car or building.

✔ If you're in the water and can see lightning, **get out immediately**. Water is a conductor for electricity. If lightning strikes the water nearby, you could be electrocuted!

✔ If there's no car or building for you to take shelter in, **go to a low-lying** (no hills!) **place away** from trees, poles or metal objects that could attract lightning. You don't want to be in a wide open space, because then *you're* the tallest thing around. Taking cover in a clump of bushes is the best place you can be.

✔ **Be a very small target.** Squat and place your hands on your knees with your head between them. Don't lie flat on the ground. This will make you a larger target.

- ✔ If you're in a group, **make sure you're at least 15 feet away from other people** so that no electric charges will transfer between you.
- ✔ If you're in the woods, **take shelter under the shortest tree you can find**.

Storm Calculator

Thunder and lightning go hand in hand. So, when you hear thunder, you know that lightning is close by and that it's time to put your guard up. To figure out how far the storm is from you, count the seconds between when you see the lightning and when you hear the thunder. Divide this number by *five*. That is roughly how many miles away the storm is from you.

Example: 5 seconds between
the lightning strike   ÷ 5   = 1 mile away
and the sound of
thunder

TAKE A HIKE

Help make your hike a happy one by being prepared *before* you hit the trails. Read on for tips on **what to wear**, smart **stuff to put in your pack**, and for some **basic hiking know-how**.

Get Ready!

How to dress (not fancy, but layered). It's best to keep your body covered when hiking in the wilderness and woods. Who knows when you might run into poison ivy, mosquitoes, prickly bushes, or even snakes! Wear long sleeves and pants, and sturdy, comfortable shoes such as hiking boots.

Get Set!

Here's what you should take with you (you can use your **HTSA survival bag** or a backpack):

- ✔ First-aid kit (see page 26 to make one)

- ✔ **HTSA whistle**

- ✔ Insect repellent

- ✔ Compass (see the survival secrets on page 13 to learn how to make one out of your watch, or how to read a real one)

- ✔ **HTSA flashlight**

- ✔ Rain gear

- ✔ Matches

- ✔ Water

- ✔ Energy snack (see a great recipe on page 12)

- ✔ An extra pair of socks

- ✔ A watch

Go!

✔ It's best to **start** hiking **early** in the day so you don't run out of light.

✔ The safest place to hike is on a trail that has been maintained (no branches or vines cluttering your way). Make sure you have a **map of your trail** and know how to read it and where you're going.

✔ It's also important to understand how much **distance** you'll cover and how long your hike will take. Remember—you still have to walk *all the way back* from your destination once you get there!

✔ **Never eat any fruits, berries, or mushrooms** you find, unless you know *exactly* what they are. They could be poisonous!

✔ **Obey all signs.** They are there for a reason.

✔ **Never go off the trail!** It's easier to get lost than you think. (You might also trample on a fragile plant or an animal's house!)

DO NOT LEAVE THE TRAIL

DO NOT FEED THE ANIMALS

✔ **Heads up!** Pay attention to your surroundings while hiking, and keep your eyes open for landmarks. It will help you retrace your steps on the way back.

✔ **Follow the leader.** Be a part of the pack and always stick with the group. Set and keep a pace everyone in the group feels comfortable with. Hiking as a group also means staying together.

Yikes! Lost in the woods...

If you get separated from your hiking crew, do this:

1. **Yell for help** and blow your whistle. Wait where you are for the group to come find you.

2. If they're too far away and don't hear you, clearly **mark the spot** where you're standing and go look for them.

3. Mark your path as you go, so you can get back to the spot you started from. **Walk for five minutes** (you don't want to get too far from your starting point) and **continue blowing your HTSA whistle** and yelling for help.

4. If you can't find your group, **go back to your starting point**, then go look in another direction. Repeat this process until you have gone north, south, east and west, using a compass or your watch as a compass.

5. If it's getting dark, **find a sheltered area for the night**. Button up and keep warm. **Send light signals** by pointing your flashlight into the treetops and repeatedly turning it off and on.

Quick Tip: People can survive weeks without food but only a few days without water!

RECIPE

Hitting the Trail Mix

Bodies need fuel to help keep them moving and energized. This salty-sweet energy snack will give your body a boost! In a resealable plastic bag, mix together **1 cup** of any of the following ingredients that you like. Shake it up and take it with you!

mixed nuts like almonds, cashews, pistachios, and peanuts

raisins or dried cranberries

granola

oat or rice cereal

M&M's

shredded coconut

pretzels

SURVIVAL SECRET

How to Read a Compass

The needle on a compass always lines up with the earth's north-south magnetic pole. So no matter which way you turn your compass, the **needle** will **still face the same way**, with the **red** part of the needle always indicating **north**. To find out which direction you are facing (or to head in the direction you want to go), hold your compass and rotate it (or yourself) until the N (north) written on the part surrounding the needle (called the *compass housing*) lines up with the North-pointing (red) side of the needle. Once you've done this, keep the compass steady and then face in the direction you would like to figure out. The letter you are lined up with (N for north, E for east, S for south or W for west) indicates the direction you are facing. If you're between two letters, then the direction you're facing is a combination of the two directions, like northeast or southwest.

ORIENTING ARROW
COMPASS NEEDLE
ORIENTING LINES
DIRECTION YOU ARE FACING

You can use your watch as a **compass**! This is how you do it (in the Northern Hemisphere):

1. Point the hour hand of your watch toward the sun.

2. Locate the **middle** space between the hour hand and twelve o'clock. That's south.

3. If it's **daylight savings time**, locate the middle space between the hour hand and eleven o'clock. Now that's **south**.

4. Once you've located south, you can identify **north**, **east**, and **west** as well.

Quick Tip:
Remember that the sun rises in the east and sets in the west.

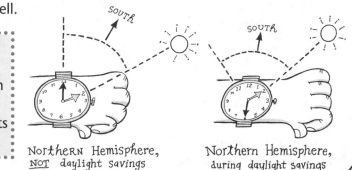

Northern Hemisphere, NOT daylight savings

Northern Hemisphere, during daylight savings

NATURE'S POISONS

Most plants and animals in nature are harmless, but there are a few pests you should watch out for. Do you know what they are and how to avoid them? Read on for ways to identify these plants and animals—and what to do if they get too close to you!

Poison ivy, poison oak, and poison sumac
When hiking, keep your eyes open for these pesky plants.

POISON IVY

POISON OAK

Poison Ivy and Poison Oak
There is an old saying "leaves of three, let them be." Both poison ivy and poison oak have three leaves per stem.

Poison Sumac
This plant has a row of six to ten leaflets. One leaflet is at the end of the stem. The others are in two rows opposite one another.

POISON SUMAC

First Aid

Symptom: The sap of poison ivy, poison oak, and poison sumac all cause a red, blister-like rash that itches and burns. You'll begin to see the rash 12 to 24 hours after you come in contact with the sap on a plant.

Remedy: Remove any clothes and shoes that have come in contact with the plant and wash them in hot water with a strong soap (if the poisonous sap is on your clothes, it can spread to you if you touch it). Keep your hands away from your face. If you've just come in contact with any of these plants, wash the affected areas with soap and cold water. If more than 30 minutes have passed, just use cold water. Dab on calamine lotion (that pink stuff) to soothe the itch and burn.

SURVIVAL SECRET
Dress in long pants, a long-sleeved shirt, and wear socks. As long as the plant doesn't touch your skin, you're safe!

Doctor, doctor!: You should call a doctor if the rash is in your mouth, nose, or around your eyes.

Snakes and Snake Bites

The good news is most snakes are **not poisonous**. But even non-poisonous snakes will bite if they feel scared. If you're hiking in an area known to have snakes, follow these steps so you don't get bitten:

- ✔ If you come upon a snake, FREEZE. Hold very still until it slithers away.

- ✔ Leave snakes alone. Many people get bitten because they try to get too close to or poke at snakes.

- ✔ Wear **long pants** and **thick boots**.

- ✔ Snakes like to hide out in small, dark places. Keep your hands and feet out of areas you can't see in.

- ✔ Stay on hiking trails and avoid tall grass where snakes can't be seen.

SURVIVAL SECRET

Snakes aren't naturally aggressive, and they only strike when they feel threatened or scared.

FROZEN PONDS

Frozen ponds are tempting to walk out on, but don't break the ice! Remember these rules for staying safe and dry.

- ✔ **Never go out on ice unless you know for sure that it's sturdy.**

- ✔ **Clear blue ice is the strongest, and it must be four inches thick to safely hold a person.** Milky, honeycombed ice that has air bubbles trapped in it is much weaker than clear blue ice.

- ✔ **Ice can be strong in some areas and not in others.** Water currents under the ice can create weak spots, so never trust ice on a river or stream.

- ✔ **Never venture out onto a snowy pond or lake.** Not only does the snow keep you from clearly seeing the ice, but it also insulates the ice and makes it harder for it to freeze solid.

If you fall through the ice...

1. Kick hard with your feet while trying to pull yourself out of the water to get back onto the ice. If you can't find the hole that you fell through, use your fists or your head to create another opening. Once you're back on the ice, roll away from the hole to shore (don't stand on the ice or you might fall through again).

2. If someone you are with has fallen in and you have a cell phone, **call 911** immediately. While you wait for help, stay on shore and lie down on your stomach. Pass them something they can use to help pull themselves onto the ice, like a branch, pole, rope, or belt.

3. Have them **roll to safety** and get medical assistance immediately. Do the same if you're the one who has fallen through the ice.

SURVIVAL SECRET

If you find yourself on thin ice and are worried about it breaking, lie down gently and roll to safety. This spreads your weight across a larger area, and reduces your risk of breaking the ice.

Frostbite!

Being out in the cold for long periods of time when not properly dressed can result in frostbite, which is when your skin and muscles actually freeze. Here's what to do to keep the frost from getting you:

✔ **Dress warmly!** Several thin layers will help keep you dry as well as warm. Don't forget to wear a hat! You lose an enormous amount of body heat by not covering your head.

✔ **Symptoms of frostbite** include numbness or pain in fingers, toes, nose, cheeks, or ears. The skin might also be blistered, hard to the touch, or glossy.

✔ **First aid for frostbite** should include the following steps:

1. **Go indoors** and call a doctor right away.

2. **Wiggle** the affected body parts to increase blood supply to the area.

3. **Warm** the frozen parts by holding them against your body.

4. **Soak** the frozen parts in warm— *not hot*— water. Frozen skin and muscle tissue are fragile and can be damaged easily.

SWIMMING SMARTS

Splish, splash, you've been waiting for the first warm day of summer—and—finally it's time to put on your swimsuit and head to the beach. Did you remember to bring your sunscreen? If not, you'll be sorry the next day when you're too sore to sit down! (When you already have a sunburn, see page 23 for how to soothe it.) But while you can, avoid the burn altogether by bringing your sunscreen with you and making sure to reapply it every couple of hours. (And don't forget that the sun's rays are just as strong when it's cloudy or overcast, even if the sun doesn't feel as hot.)

Now, what if you're taking a dip when all of a sudden the tides turn? Here's some help for the next time you find yourself in the water and in need of help.

First off: Don't ever swim by yourself or in an area where there's no lifeguard, or that's off-limits to swimmers.

You get a cramp while swimming

Signal to someone nearby that you need help. Then lie back and float. Massage the cramping area and take deep breaths. If there is no one to help you, wait for the cramping to ease, then swim to shore.

Tip: *To help prevent cramps, you should always wait 30 minutes after eating to let food digest before swimming.*

The undertow is stronger than you are

An undertow is the strong current that pulls the water back out to sea after a wave breaks. Usually the undertow isn't a big deal, but sometimes it can be stronger than you think. If you find yourself caught in one, don't waste your energy trying to fight it by swimming straight toward shore. Swim parallel to the shore instead. When the current relaxes, swim toward the beach. **Tip:** *Warning—the bigger the waves, the stronger the undertow!*

SWIM PARALLEL TO SHORE!

RIPTIDE

You swim out too far and you're too tired to get back

Stay calm. You need to save your energy, and panicking uses a lot of it. If there are people within sight, signal to them that you need help. Swim with your **HTSA glow-in-the-dark whistle** around your wrist so that you can use it to call for help if necessary. (Notice that a lifeguard always wears a whistle so that s/he can warn a swimmer who is out too far to swim closer to shore.) Take a rest by floating on your back. If there's no one to help you, wait until you feel stronger, then swim to shore using a relaxing stroke like the backstroke or breaststroke. **Tip:** *Know your limits. Remember, swimming out is only half the journey—you still have to swim back in!*

BACKSTROKE TO SHORE

SURVIVAL SECRET

Never swim alone. Always take a buddy with you so they can call for help if you need it. And always swim in an area where only swimming is permitted, and which has lifeguards.

Swimming with the Big Boats

Warning: Stay alert while swimming in crowded lakes. Watch out for water-skiers and boats. Remember, you're a little, bobbing head in the water. Just because *you* see them doesn't mean they see you!

BEACH BAG BASICS

When you head to the beach, be sure to pack your beach towels and buckets, but don't forget to add these basics, too:

FIRST AID KIT

WATER BOTTLE

BEACH TOWELS

LIP BALM

BUCKETS

SUNSCREEN

SUNHAT

SUNGLASSES

DRY CLOTHES

LONG-SLEEVED SHIRT

Tip: *Carry these beach bag basics in your HTSA survival bag!*

FIRST AID! FROM QUICK FIXES TO BROKEN BONES...

Stinging scrapes, cuts or stings. Here are tips for treating all kinds of pains—little and big.

	SYMPTOM	REMEDY	DOCTOR! DOCTOR!
Hiccups	An uncontrollable sucking in of air in short, quick breaths.	To stop hiccups, hold your breath or blow into a paper bag (not plastic). Other methods to try are drinking a glass of water slowly or sucking on ice.	Call the doctor if the hiccups last more than a couple hours.
Bee Sting	It hurts! The area around the sting will also become red and swollen.	Bees leave behind a stinger. Don't try to pull out a stinger because this could cause it to release more venom (that's what makes it hurt). Instead, try to gently scrape out the stinger by using a blunt-edged object, like a credit card. Soothe the sting by washing the area with soap and water. Then apply an ice pack for a few minutes. If you can, make a paste using a spoonful of baking soda and a couple drops of water. Apply it to the area and leave it on for 15 minutes.	Seek medical attention immediately if you get stung in the mouth or nose. Swelling could block your air passages. Also call a doctor if you have a hard time breathing, feel dizzy, get hives, or feel tight in your throat and chest—this could mean you're having an allergic reaction.

	SYMPTOM	REMEDY	DOCTOR! DOCTOR!
Mosquito Bite	An itchy bump that could be red or white.	To help relieve the itching, apply a cool compress (like a cold, damp washcloth, an ice pack wrapped in a towel, or ice cubes in a resealable plastic bag) to the area, then dab calamine lotion on the bite.	Extreme scratching may cause infection. If the mosquito bite is oozing, swollen, or irritated after a few days, call your doctor.
Cuts	An open wound often accompanied by bleeding.	Apply pressure for 10 minutes to stop bleeding. Gently wash the wound with soap and warm water. To remove dirt, lightly scrub the area with a clean cloth. Apply an antibiotic ointment to help fight infection, and cover it with a band-aid. Change your band-aid every day until a scab forms. *Never pick at scabs.* They are your body's way of protecting a wound while it heals. Picking just slows the process down, and could leave you with a permanent scar.	You may need stitches if the cut is very wide or deep, doesn't stop bleeding, or can't be held together by a band-aid.

	SYMPTOM	REMEDY	DOCTOR! DOCTOR!
Sunburn	Your skin will become red and warm to the touch. It will also be very tender.	Apply a cool compress for 10 to 15 minutes throughout the day, or soak in a cool bath. A few spoonfuls of baking soda added to your bath water will help ease the pain. Apply a body lotion, or aloe vera gel to the affected area to moisturize and soothe the burn.	If the sunburn is very severe, and accompanied by nausea, fever, chills, or blisters, you should call a doctor.
Heat Stroke	Heat stroke is caused by a combination of too much sun and heat! Symptoms may include headache, dizziness, confusion, and rapid heartbeat.	Go indoors and lie down with your feet slightly elevated. Loosen your clothing and gently apply a cool, damp compress to your skin. Drink lots of water.	If you still feel really sick after several minutes in a cool spot, call a doctor.

	SYMPTOM	REMEDY	DOCTOR! DOCTOR!
Nose-bleeds	Blood oozing from your nostrils.	Sit up with your head bent forward so that you're looking down. Clamp your nose closed with your fingers for five minutes and breathe through your mouth. At the same time, apply a cold compress to the back of your neck or your forehead. If bleeding starts up again, repeat this process.	If you get lots of nosebleeds, you could have allergies. A trip to the doctor would help.
Strains and Sprains	When you over-do it physically, you may experience sudden pain in a joint or muscle. A *sprain* is the stretching or tearing of the ligaments, the tissues that connect the bones. A *strain* is a stretching or tearing of the muscle.	Apply ice to the area to help reduce swelling. Put as little pressure as possible on the hurt area.	If you have a severe sprain or strain, your doctor may immobilize the area with a splint.

	SYMPTOM	REMEDY	DOCTOR! DOCTOR!
Bruises	A bruise is caused by bleeding beneath the skin. The hurt area will turn purple or greenish in color.	Apply an ice pack for 20 minutes to stop the bleeding. After 48 hours, apply a warm washcloth for 10 minutes a day to help reabsorb the blood.	If the pain increases over time or the bruise doesn't heal, see a doctor.
Broken Bone	You may hear a pop or some other sound your limb doesn't normally make. You will also have extreme pain at the site of the injury, and won't be able to use the broken limb.	Get medical help immediately. Don't try to use the broken limb and don't move it. Use a clean, dry cloth to cover it until medical help arrives.	A doctor will take X-rays and put the bone back in place, then secure it with a cast or splint.

PROJECT

First-Aid Tools

A first-aid kit packed with all the right stuff and a quick lesson in how to make a sling will help you be prepared for pain emergencies.

Make a First-Aid Kit

Pack these items in a plastic container with a lid or in a sealable bag. Then slip it in your **HTSA survival bag** and you're ready to go.

- ✔ Band-aids
- ✔ Cotton balls
- ✔ Gauze and tape
- ✔ Small bottle of rubbing alcohol to clean and sterilize cuts (use antiseptic spray or a small bottle of hydrogen peroxide as substitutes)
- ✔ Ibuprofen or aspirin
- ✔ Tweezers

- ✔ Insect repellent
- ✔ Decongestant
- ✔ Antibiotic lotion
- ✔ Small pair of scissors
- ✔ Ace bandage
- ✔ Safety pins
- ✔ Antibacterial hand gel (for when you don't have soap and water)

Make a Sling

Moving a wounded arm can cause more pain and injury. To help keep the arm steady, follow these directions for making a sling.

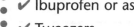

ELBOW AT TOP POINT OF TRIANGLE

1. A piece of cloth cut in the shape of a triangle is the best thing to use. It should be large enough to tie over your shoulder with a loose pouch for holding your arm. If no cloth is available, you can use a belt, shirt, pants or a rope.

2. Place the injured arm inside the sling with the elbow at the top point of the triangle.

3. Bring the two free points up to the opposite shoulder. Adjust the height so the elbow is at a right angle and pin or tie the sling together.

The Great Indoors (And City Life)

Here's how to deal with all sorts of challenges from getting lost on city streets to knowing how to protect yourself in your own home or apartment.

HOW TO SURVIVE THE CITY

LOST IN A STRANGE PLACE

Stop! If you get separated from friends or family, do this:

1. **Stay close to the spot you saw them last.** It will probably be the first place they check. If you go looking for them while they're looking for you, there's a good chance you'll miss one another!

2. If you don't feel safe waiting in the spot you last saw them, **find a public place close by where you do feel safe**, like a store, restaurant, or office building. *Don't* accept a stranger's offer for a ride, or to walk you someplace. It's safer to be around lots of people than alone with just one person, especially someone you don't know.

3. **Find a phone** and either call the cell phone of someone in your group, or call the place where you're staying. If no one answers, leave a detailed message explaining where you are so they can come get you.

4. **If you have money for a cab** and have waited for a while but haven't been found, go to the place where you're staying.

SURVIVAL SECRET

Before going out and about, do this:

✔ Write down the address and phone number of where you're staying and tuck it in your wallet or **HTSA cash stash**.

✔ Bring enough money to take a cab back to where you're staying and some spare change for a pay phone (even if you have a cell phone, because it doesn't always work).

✔ Agree on a meeting place in case someone should get separated.

GETTING AROUND TOWN

Being able to navigate your city or town using public transportation is important for city survival. Make sure you have some change in your **HTSA cash stash** so that you can get where you need to go! Though bus and train timetables and maps are different from town to town, there are some basic things they have in common. Here are three things you need to know:

a. The name of the station where you are now

b. The name of the station you want to get to

c. The "color line" or "route number" you need to take

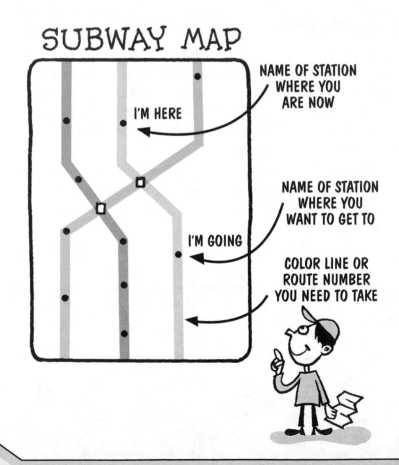

SUBWAY MAP

I'M HERE → NAME OF STATION WHERE YOU ARE NOW

I'M GOING → NAME OF STATION WHERE YOU WANT TO GET TO

COLOR LINE OR ROUTE NUMBER YOU NEED TO TAKE

Riding the subway

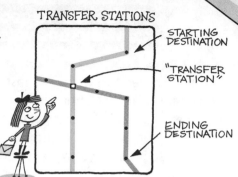

1. There are many **lines**, or routes, that make up a subway system. Most have their own color and number. Using your subway map, locate the station where you are now and the station you want to get to.

2. Then find the colored line that connects them. Sometimes it will take more than one train to get to your destination. This means you have to **transfer** to a different colored line.

3. **Locate a station where transfers can be made.** You can get off the subway train for any of the lines that stop at that station and switch to another line. You usually won't have to pay again, but you will probably have to walk to another platform to catch your new train. If so, look for the signs that show your color line and follow them, or find an information booth and ask.

Riding the bus

1. Just like the subway system has colored lines to help you navigate, buses have route numbers. The **route numbers** of the buses that stop there will be listed on the sign at the bus stop.

2. Most signs will also display a route map and bus schedule. Be sure to check the bus schedule, because it can be different during the week than it is on Saturdays, Sundays, and holidays.

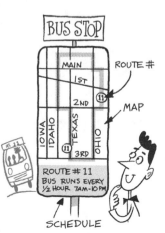

3. **Before you board a bus**, check to make sure it's the right route number. The route number will be clearly displayed on the front and sides of the bus. Once you board, you can double-check the route by asking the driver if the bus stops at your destination, and how many stops until you get there.

4. **When the driver announces your stop**, pull the cord above your head or press the stop-request bar (different buses have different signals) to let the driver know you want to get off at that stop.

What is an express train or bus?

These buses and trains are faster because they skip certain subway stations or bus stops. Check to see if an express train or bus stops at your destination *before* getting on one. You'll know it's an express train or bus because it will say "Express" on it, or on the sign on the subway platform.

How will I know when it's my subway or bus stop?

The conductor or bus driver will usually announce the name of the next stop before arriving. It's a good idea to know the names of the stops right before and after your stop so you're prepared to get off when you arrive at your stop (or know when you've gone too far!). Don't worry if you didn't hear the conductor (and don't rely on the conductor)—the station names are clearly marked on signs at each subway station, and street signs are easy to see from the bus. So watch out the window.

What if I miss my subway stop or get on the wrong train?

Once you realize your mistake, get off the train at the next stop. Check your subway map or ask for help at an information booth. No matter how far you travel or how many times you transfer, as long as you don't pass through the turnstile gates, you usually won't have to pay again.

What if I get on the wrong bus or miss my stop?

Ask the driver for help. He can tell you how to transfer to the right bus. Don't get off the bus in a strange neighborhood, especially if you don't know how to get where you're going from there.

SURVIVAL SECRET

Look online for public transportation maps and schedules for your city so you can plan your route and check the times *before* you go.

STRANGER DANGER: IF YOU'RE BEING FOLLOWED

You're starting to get a weird feeling in the pit of your stomach—the same man has been walking behind you—maybe following you—for blocks. But he looks harmless....

1. If you suspect (even just a little bit) that you're being followed, **get help immediately**. Walk into the nearest store, gas station, or restaurant and let someone know.

2. **Don't take short cuts** through deserted areas such as alleys or behind buildings where you can't easily be seen or heard. Stay in well-lit, public areas.

3. If you're in a quiet area, **stay in open spaces**. Walk (carefully, of course!) in the street if you have to. If someone helpful (like a police officer) *does* happen to walk or drive by, they can see you.

4. If there's no one around to help and you have a **cell phone**, use it! Keep on walking and call 911! (Be sure to carry your **HTSA whistle** with you, and use it to help sound the alarm.)

5. If the person corners you and asks for your valuables, **give them what they want**.

6. **Never get too close** to a car with a stranger in it. They could pull you into the car. If the car starts to follow you, turn and run in the opposite direction (it takes a lot of time for a car to turn around and follow you).

SURVIVAL SECRET

If a stranger tries to grab you, fall to the ground—scream, kick, bite, blow your **HTSA whistle**—do anything you can to attract attention and get away.

Walk Wise

- **Don't** walk alone after dark.
- **Don't** take shortcuts through deserted areas.
- **Do** let someone know where you're going, especially if you're alone.
- **Do** keep valuables out of sight (hide money in your **HTSA cash stash**).
- **Do** bring your cell phone and the **HTSA whistle** from your survival pack.

- **Do** trust your feelings. If you feel scared, go to a safe place and get help. Even if you aren't being followed, it's "better safe than sorry."
- **Do** remember that the average car weighs about 3,000 pounds. That is to say, don't dart out in front of one!
- **Don't** be afraid to run or shout for help if you feel you need to.

Cell Phone Savvy

Cell phones are a great thing to have in an emergency. Even if you're just going to be out and about for the afternoon, it's a good idea to take it along.

1. Before leaving the house, **make sure that your phone is fully charged**. Carry an extra battery just in case.

2. Don't misuse it. **Reserve cell phone power** in case you really *need* to make a call.

3. Program 911 and other important numbers, like your parent's cell phone and work numbers, into speed dial. (But still have those numbers memorized in case you need to call from a different phone.)

4. **Don't bury your phone at the bottom of your bag.** Keep it handy just in case you need to get to it quickly.

5. **Don't talk so loud that strangers can hear your personal information**, like that your parents aren't home.

6. **Don't get so involved in a conversation that you stop paying attention to what's going on around you.** It's best to be in a quiet, stationary place when you're having a conversation.

Tip: *A great place to keep your cell phone is in one of the outside pockets of your HTSA survival bag.*

BLAH BLAH BLAH...

HONK!

STREETWISE...

Do you know the rules of the road, how to read a subway map, or what to do if a stranger is following you?

Read on for smart tips to getting around safely.

PoP QuiZ — Road Rules

Whether you're on a **bike**, **rollerblades**, a **skateboard**, or **scooter**, or just **walking** the rules of the road are all the same. Do you know what to do? Answer **true** or **false** and find out.

1. When riding your wheels on the sidewalk, pedestrians have the right of way.

T   F

2. In the street, you're supposed to ride in the same direction as traffic, not against it.

T   F

3. When making a turn, use your hand to point in the direction of your turn.

T   F

4. Obey all traffic regulations. Anything a car must do (like stop at a red light), you must do, too.

T   F

5. Bright-colored clothes help make you more visible, especially at night.

T   F

6. If you have to pass, always pass someone on their left. You should announce your intentions to people by saying "passing on the left."

T   F

7. You should ride (or walk) so drivers can see you and predict your movements.

T   F

8. Be alert, on the defense, and expect the unexpected.

T   F

Answer Key: If you answered all **TRUE**, you aced the quiz! Give yourself an A+ and feel confident that your traffic law knowledge will keep you—and others—safe. Did you MISS ONE or two, or even a few? Go back and review the ones you got wrong. Safety is easy to learn.

34

You're home. Now what? What do you do if you're home alone and...you get locked out? a thunderstorm rolls in? you think an intruder is in the house? Read on to find out.

HOME ALONE BASICS

Feeling safe is feeling confident. Check out these basic tips for ways to handle prying phone callers, a stranger at the door, and being locked out.

Phone time

✔ Call a parent as soon as you arrive so they know you got home safely and everything is OK.

✔ Have a list of emergency numbers posted just in case you can't reach a parent. And don't forget, you can always call 911!

If you answer the phone, never tell a stranger that you're alone, or give out any personal information, like your name, address, or age. If they ask for your mom or dad, simply tell the person your mom or dad can't come to the phone right now. Offer to take a message instead. If you have an answering machine, it's often best to let it answer for you. If the call is for you, you can always pick up.

Stranger at the door

✔ When you're home alone, keep the door locked at all times. Never open it if you don't know the person or if you're not expecting anyone.

Locked out!

✔ In case you're locked out, it's always a good idea to have a spare key hidden, or to have given a key to a friend or neighbor ahead of time for just such a situation (and don't

forget to return the key so that they'll have it the next time you need it). Never try to break into your home—you could get hurt or damage something.

✔ If you can't get into your home and you decide to leave, put a note on the door (or, if you have a cell phone, call) to let a parent or other adult know where you'll be. If you have a phone, call a parent and let them know your plans.

✔ If you get home and see that something is wrong, like a window is broken or a door is standing open, don't go inside. Go to a neighbor for help.

BATTERY ☑
SMOKE ALARM ☑
WINDOW, DOOR LOCKS ☑
PEEPHOLE ☑
FUSE BOX ☑

PROJECT

Safe Home Checklist

Do this: Check your house and make sure that it has all of the items listed below, that they are in good working order, and that you know how to use them. Check off each item on your list if you have it and you know how it works. If you don't understand what to do or how to use it, have a parent show you.

○ **HTSA flashlight**

○ Spare batteries for the flashlight

○ Smoke alarms

○ Locks on windows and doors

○ Peephole or window on the front door so visitors can be identified. If there is no peephole on your door, look for a window (with curtains) nearby that you can peek through instead.

○ Fuse box

WHEN THE POWER GOES OUT

You're in your kitchen making an after-school snack while singing along to your favorite CD, or watching TV, when all of a sudden, the music stops, the TV goes silent, and the lights go out. Blackout time! Prepare yourself for lights-out by following these tips:

Be prepared:

- Do you have an extra **battery-operated radio** and your **HTSA flashlight**? Do you know where they are? And *most* important, do the batteries work?

- Is your cell phone charged?

- Do you have enough bottled water in the house to last you and the members of your household at least three days? (A gallon per person per day is a good estimate.)

Make sure you can answer these questions with a **"yes!"** *anytime* you're asked.

When the power goes out:

- **Fill up some containers** (and maybe your bathtub, too) **with water** (in case the water turns off in a few hours and you need it for washing up).

- **Turn off the switches** to anything on before the power went out (lights, fans, computer, TV, radio). Otherwise, a fuse might blow when the power is restored.

- **Don't open the fridge too much** (especially if you're opening it because it's cool and you're hot!). The more you open it, the faster your food will spoil. An unopened freezer will keep food cold for up to 36 hours.

- Make sure you **drink plenty of water.** Save energy by limiting activity—keep yourself cool if the weather is hot by opening the windows. If it's cold, bundle up under some blankets and think warm thoughts or jump around a bit.

- Sometimes the phone lines still work. *Don't* tie them up with silly calls. *Do* call a parent to let them know the power is out (so they can pick up hot dinner and any other supplies you might need on the way home).

- If the power outage is affecting a large area of land, your parents may be stuck in traffic or on public transportation, so don't worry if they're a little late getting home.

- If you have a cell phone, it's probably still working. Again, don't waste the batteries on unnecessary calls.

RECIPE

Pop & Top:

Put 3 cups pre-popped popcorn in a resealable plastic bag. Add 2 tablespoons of any one of the following flavorings: taco seasoning, Parmesan cheese, mini marshmallows, peanuts, or raisins. Then shake it up!

In the Dark

Power outages happen most often in really hot and humid weather (because too many people are running their air conditioners full blast). You can help prevent outages by making sure you turn the lights and AC off and by making sure the refrigerator door is closed tightly whenever you're not using it.

DURING A THUNDERSTORM

The sky is getting darker, the wind starts howling, and the thunder is so loud your dog has taken cover under the couch. If you're home alone and it begins to storm, follow these tips for staying safe inside:

- **Don't handle any electrical equipment or phones.** Lightning can hit power and phone lines, sending electricity through the wires to your home.

- **Avoid taking a bath or shower**, or turning on the faucet for any other purpose. Metal pipes can transmit electricity, too.

- **Turn off your computer.** Power surges from lightning can cause a lot of damage to computer hardware.

- If it's really windy, **close the windows,** and curtains or shades.

- **Find a flashlight** in case the power goes out. Use your **HTSA flashlight** and listen to the news on a battery-operated radio to learn more about the storm.

- **If you're scared, do something to distract yourself.** Now is the time to sing at the top of your lungs, off-key, and no one will mind (or hear)!

> **Quick Tip:** See page 8 for more information on thunderstorms and what to do if you're caught outside in one. See page 37 for more information about dealing with power outages!

AT HOME POISONS

You already know that being able to recognize poisonous plants can save you a lot of pain when you're outside (see page 14), but knowing what poisons to avoid when you're *inside* is just as important. Here's what you need to know about how to prevent everyday things in your home from making you sick.

Stuff you might not ever think of as poisonous—such as glue, medicine, cleaning products, and paint can make you really sick if you accidentally swallow them, get them in your eyes, or inhale their fumes.

✔ If you're using a product like superglue, rubber cement, turpentine, or paint to fix something for art projects, **stay in a well-ventilated area** (open lots of windows!). Also, always close the lid when you're not actually using the goop.

✔ **Read the directions before using anything.** Follow them.

✔ **Keep poisonous products away from younger siblings** and their friends, and never leave little children unsupervised.

✔ **Stay away from areas under construction**—paint and other building materials release all sorts of poisonous chemicals (and most of them you can't see or smell).

✔ **Ask your parents to get a carbon monoxide monitor** (carbon monoxide is a gas you can't see, taste, or smell, but it's *really* dangerous).

If you or someone in your house does touch, inhale, or swallow something you think is poisonous (there's usually a poison warning label), here's what to do:

✔ **Call your local poison center** (or 911) immediately. The national poison center hotline is: 1-800-222-1222. While you're waiting for help:

- If the **poison** was **swallowed**, don't give the victim anything to eat or drink before calling the poison center.

- If the **poison** was **inhaled**, get the victim to fresh air right away.

- If the **poison** is on the **skin**, wash the affected area for 10 minutes.

- If the **poison** is in the **eye**, use a large cup filled with warm water held about 4 inches from the eye for 15 minutes to flush it out.

Gas Leaks

If you smell or hear gas escaping from a broken line:

- **Get out** of the house **immediately**.

- Call a parent to let them know. Then go to a neighbor's house and call the gas company to let them know the problem (your parent can do this, too).

- **Don't turn on or off any lights**, or use a phone (regular or cellular), or anything electrical. Sparks can make the leaking gas catch fire.

- **Leave as many doors and windows open as possible**—this will help get the poisonous fumes out.

SURF SMART

Whether it's a stranger on the street, a stranger on the phone, or a stranger online, the same rules apply. **Make the most of your time on the Internet by surfing safe and smart.** Check out the tips below for doing so!

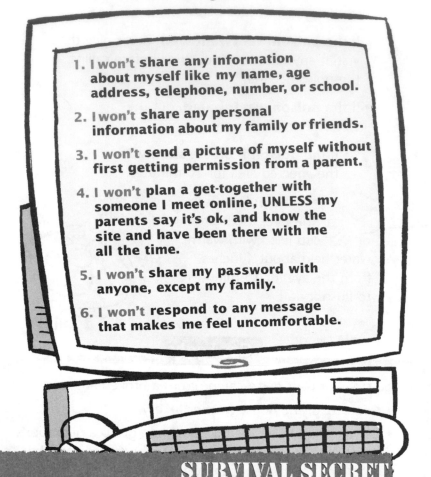

1. I won't **share any information about myself like my name, age address, telephone, number, or school.**

2. I won't **share any personal information about my family or friends.**

3. I won't **send a picture of myself without first getting permission from a parent.**

4. I won't **plan a get-together with someone I meet online, UNLESS my parents say it's ok, and know the site and have been there with me all the time.**

5. I won't **share my password with anyone, except my family.**

6. I won't **respond to any message that makes me feel uncomfortable.**

SURVIVAL SECRET

If there is only one phone line in your home, talk with your parents ahead of time and agree on a time you can be online and for how long. That way if they need to reach you when you're home alone, they can. Here's when having a cell phone also comes in handy. If you have one and your parents have one, and you have only one phone line, they can still reach you (and you them) while you're online.

ometimes you'll bump into situations that are so much BIGGER than you are that you can't avoid them or fix them. But as a smart survivor, you can use your skills to deal with them in the best way possible.

FIRE! FIRE!

If there's a fire in your home or in your apartment building or the building you are in, the most important thing to do is **get out quickly**.

Follow this list of do's and don'ts for getting out.

1. **Don't** take the time to collect your belongings, no matter how important they may be. **Yes, that means pets, too.**

2. Smoke rises, so it's best to stay low. **Do** get down on all fours and crawl to safety.

3. **Don't** open any door without feeling it first. Doorknobs can get so hot they burn your hand, and if it's hot, it means the fire is burning on the other side. Try to find another way out.

4. **Once you're safely out of a room where the fire is, close the door behind you so the fire doesn't spread to other rooms or to other floors.**

5. **Do** have a family plan and pick a safe and easy place for everyone to meet after they get out.

6. Once out of the house, **call 911** immediately.

SURVIVAL SECRET

If your clothes catch on fire, Stop, Drop, and Roll:

1. **Stop!** Don't run around, it will only fuel the fire.

2. **Drop** to the ground and stretch out long. Protect your face with your hands.

3. **Roll** to put out the flames.

Fire Escape: Map out your route!

Fires are scary and confusing, and heavy smoke can make rooms so dark you won't be able to see. Map your route out now, so you can escape quickly, and practice following that route with your family.

You will need:

A separate piece of paper for each floor of your house or apartment	A different colored pen or marker for each room on your map

1. Draw the rooms of your house. Make sure to add all windows and doors.

2. Select a colored pen for each room. Write in the name of the room using that color.

3. Try to find two ways out from every room in your house. Using the room's specific color pen, draw arrows leading from that room out of the house.

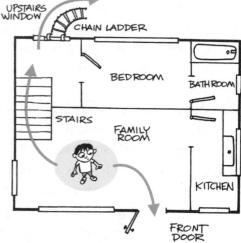

4. If the alternative escape route is from a window on a higher floor, make sure you draw in a chain fire ladder. This is an emergency ladder that can be stored in a closet or under a bed until it's needed. Practice with your family securing the ladder in the window so you know how it works (just in case!) and practice climbing down it, too.

STUCK IN AN ELEVATOR

Luckily, elevators don't get stuck very often or for very long. But just in case you're in one that *does* S-T-O-P in the middle of your ride, do this:

1. Look for the red **emergency button** on the button panel. Push it and an alarm will sound.

2. Some elevators have **phones** in them for emergency situations. If you're in an elevator that has one, follow the directions and use it to contact help.

3. If you have a **cell phone**, you can try using it to contact a parent or 911. But often cell phones don't work very well in elevators.

4. **Wait.** A stuck elevator doesn't usually go unnoticed for long.

EVACUATING A BUILDING

From fires to blackouts, here are tips for keeping your cool while evacuating a building in an emergency:

✔ **Stay calm.** Don't waste your energy on panic, that's not going to help. Focus **on getting out** safely instead.

✔ **Use your head.** Act—don't react! Take a moment to try to **understand the situation** and your **safest options** for evacuating. If you have a cell phone, call 911!

✔ **Look for the nearest exit.** Always take the **stairs**, never an elevator!

✔ **Follow the leader.** If a knowledgeable adult has taken charge, do as they say. This is not the time to strike out on your own.

PROJECT

Make a Home Emergency Kit

From fires to floods, be prepared for anything! Pack up these survival tools in a small duffel bag or knapsack, or in your **HTSA survival bag**. Keep it in a handy place just in case you have to grab it and go—or stay!

- ○ **HTSA flashlight** with spare batteries
- ○ Small battery-operated radio
- ○ Bottled water
- ○ Packaged snacks, like crackers or cereal
- ○ Cloths for covering your face
- ○ Blankets
- ○ First-aid kit (see page 26 to make one)
- ○ **HTSA whistle**

The Tough Stuff: From Bullies to Blunders to Bloopers

This section will show you how to handle stuff that just happens—from getting caught with your zipper down to dropping your lunch tray in front of everybody in the cafeteria.

HOW TO SURVIVE MEANIES...

Meanness is often a cover up for something else, like insecurity. Understanding what makes meanies—like bullies—tick will also help you understand how to handle the situation.

YOU'RE PICKED ON BY A BULLY

Try these three ways to make a bully go away...

> MY BABY SISTER IS STRONGER THAN YOU

1. **Ignore the bully.** Don't say a word. If he can't get a rise out of you, he may eventually get bored and leave you alone.

> YOUR BREATH SMELLS LIKE YOUR DOG'S

> I BRUSH HIS TEETH EVERYDAY

2. **Use reverse psychology** (that means doing the opposite of what someone thinks you'll do) and turn their insults into compliments.

> YOU'RE WEIRD

> THANKS FOR APPRECIATING MY UNIQUE QUALITIES

3. **Agree with them.** It will probably leave them momentarily speechless and certainly takes the fun out of the taunt.

SURVIVAL SECRET

Sometimes someone acts mean because they feel **angry**, **hurt**, or **afraid**. It helps them feel powerful. When someone is acting like a bully, there is probably a sad, frightened person inside who likely is being bullied by someone—just as s/he is bullying you!

47

YOU'RE THREATENED BY A DOG

Most ferociously barking dogs aren't really as mean as they seem—they're scared. If you're approached by a threatening dog, do this:

1. **If a dog is running at you full speed**, he's not necessarily mean—he may just want to play.

2. **Never scream and run!** You will only trigger the dog's chase response. Just like a dog will chase a ball or stick—it'll chase you, too. (And it's almost impossible to outrun a dog!)

3. **Don't look the dog in the eyes.** Dogs find this threatening and could feel challenged to attack.

4. **Be a tree**. Stand very quietly and still with your hands at your sides until the dog leaves.

5. **Let the dog sniff you.** Chances are it will realize you aren't a threat and leave you alone.

6. **Back away very slowly** until the dog is out of sight. Don't turn your back on him.

7. **If the dog should try to attack you** (because after all is said and done, there *are* some dogs who are just mean—possibly because they have been mistreated) give it something else to bite, like your knapsack (your **HTSA survival bag**, if you're carrying it) or jacket. If the dog knocks you over, curl into a tight ball with your face down to the ground and cover your ears with your hands.

SURVIVAL SECRET

Even though you want to run, don't! Standing still or backing away is the best way to prevent a dog from attacking. After all, if it has nothing to chase after, it won't chase!

YOU STRIKE OUT WHEN THE TEAM IS DEPENDING ON YOU

It's the ninth inning, your team has two outs, and the bases are loaded. It's your big moment, your chance to shine... then *whoosh, whoosh, whoosh*—three strikes and you're out! And the other team wins.

Have you ever felt like you let down your whole team by losing the game with one bad play? There's no need to throw the bat, stomp off the field, or pick a fight with the umpire. Just take a deep breath, hold your head high, and **be strong**. Now turn around and **face** your teammates. Yes, they're disappointed. So are you! Let them know you're **sorry**, but **don't dwell** on it. Winning or losing the game may come down to one final play, but there are **many** plays throughout a game that bring you to that point. Remember, you probably weren't the only person to strike out, miss the catch, or get caught stealing a base! So **move on**. Think about the **good** defensive **plays you've made**, like how you robbed the other team of a base hit, and the other good offensive moves you had (remember your last hit or basket or goal). Go easy on yourself. Hang out with your family, best friend, or dog. *They* won't hold it against you if you missed scoring the winning run!

SURVIVAL SECRET

Just like it takes a whole team to win a game, it takes a whole team to lose one, too.

YOU'RE CAUGHT WITH YOUR ZIPPER DOWN

Sound familiar? This can happen to anyone. Here's what you do!

No need to win the **red face** award for this little slip. Simply say, "Excuse me," then turn around and discreetly **zip your fly**. Then go on with your day.

OOPS! EXCUSE ME WHILE I TAKE CARE OF A LITTLE BUSINESS!

SURVIVAL SECRET
What's the big deal? Who *hasn't* forgotten to zip up his pants at least once, or had a zipper that slipped?

YOU TRIP AND FALL IN FRONT OF THE WHOLE SCHOOL

It's the moment that everybody dreads, a worst nightmare come true—the big CRASH, TRIP, PLOP in front of a crowd. How could it happen to you? Because it happens to *lots* of people, that's how! The important thing is to make sure you're not hurt. Then, stand up and straighten yourself out. So maybe there are a few snickers from the crowd. If you're feeling brave, crack a joke. Otherwise, brush yourself off and move along. Make yourself feel better by thinking about how much more embarrassing the situation *could* have been—like if you'd thrown up in front of the whole school (see page 51 for dealing with that, too)!

SURVIVAL SECRET
Don't take the snickers personally. Sometimes, because your fall is so unexpected, it just *looks* funny. The other kids aren't really laughing at you (they'd laugh at anyone, and you might too, if it were someone else). Laugh along with the others, if you can manage it.

YOU THROW UP AT SCHOOL

It's gross *and* embarrassing. Should you go into hiding or deal with the mess right away? Neither! Do this instead:

1. Ignore the mess and **take care of yourself first**. Go to the bathroom and rinse out your mouth. If you got any vomit on yourself, use a damp towel and a little bit of soap to dab off the spots.

2. **Go to the nurse's office.** Chances are you're not feeling so hot.

3. Feeling embarrassed? Forget it. After all, **it could happen to anybody**. Think about it. Do you remember it ever happening to someone else? Focus on getting better, and put the episode behind you. If you do, others will too.

SURVIVAL SECRET
Remember, you're not the only one who has ever thrown up!

YOU LAUGH SO HARD YOU SPEW MILK ON YOUR FRIEND

You're sitting at the lunch table with a bunch of pals and your best friend tells a joke just as you're taking a sip of milk. In it goes…and out it comes! The person sitting next to you has just received a **milk shower**. Chances are everyone will think this is pretty funny…except the person covered in milk. **Don't** just **sit there and laugh** at your friend or be embarrassed—offer your napkin so she can **clean** up. If you need to, excuse yourselves and go to the bathroom. Use soap and water to finish the job. **Say you're sorry**; it was an **accident**.

SURVIVAL SECRET
When you and your friends are being silly, try to keep your laughs between sips of milk or, better yet, when you're not eating or drinking.

YOU'RE THE LAST PERSON CHOSEN FOR THE TEAM

1. It's situations like this that test the **strength of your character**. There is no way out of it; you must simply endure.

2. Say to yourself, **"I will not take it personally."** This isn't a popularity contest. It has nothing to do with anything except how good you are at the game they're choosing teams for. Perhaps they've never even seen you play and don't have a clue how good you are...or how much potential you have to be a good player!

3. Maybe this just isn't your sport. Instead of sitting there feeling miserable and wishing you were a better player, remind yourself of the **things you *are* good at**.

4. When you *do* get selected, be a good sport. Don't act bummed out, annoyed, or even too cool for your own good. Do your best to smile, hold your head up, and go join your team.

SURVIVAL SECRET
No one is good at *everything*, but...
practice + more practice = improvement!

YOU'RE CAUGHT IN A LIE

Someone took a $5 bill from your brother's piggy bank. You promise that it wasn't you, but your little sister saw you do it— and she told on you. The cat's out of the bag, so what are you going to do now?

1. **The truth is out**—and you didn't tell it. You might feel **ashamed or embarrassed. Be strong.** What's done is done, and you can't change that. Now, do what you can to **make the situation right** (or at least make things better).

2. **Be honest.** Admit that you lied. Not only is it the right thing to do, but it's also the **smart** thing to do. The more you try to cover up, the messier the situation gets (and the sillier you look). Your only hope for saving face is to **tell the truth!**

3. **Accept the blame.** Don't make excuses or try to pin it on someone else. That's a slimy thing to do. Take responsibility for your own actions. If nothing else, people will respect the way you've handled the situation (even if you didn't admit the truth right away).

4. **Say you're sorry.** It's important to let others know that you feel bad about what you did.

5. **Make it right.** Is there something you can do to make the situation better, like pay back the five dollars *and* help your brother rake the yard as a way of showing you're sorry? Find a way—and do it.

6. **Accept the consequences.** It may take a while for the people hurt by your lie to trust you again. Depending on the situation, broken trust can take time to mend.

SURVIVAL SECRET
You *can't* take back your lie, but you *can* earn respect by owning up to what you did.

YUCK! GAG! YOU JUST ATE SOMETHING YOU WISH YOU HADN'T

Try not to make a horrible face—you don't want to hurt the cook's feelings. Chew slowly, and if possible, swallow it in one big gulp. If you truly think it might make you sick, cover your mouth with your napkin and quietly spit it out. Fold your napkin to cover the chewed-up food and place it back in your lap. Eat around the food you dislike, and if you're offered seconds, politely say "No thank you."

Oops! Spilled Milk

Don't cry over spilled milk (or juice or soda or whatever)! Accidents happen to everyone. Apologize and offer to help clean up. If you have a paper or cloth napkin, use it to absorb some of the spill. If there's a tablecloth, use your napkin and push down on the spill to absorb it—don't rub.

Blot that spot! (Or, what to do when you stain your shirt)

1. Dampen a clean paper towel or cloth with water. Press it into the spill—don't rub.

2. Add a little soap to your towel, if needed, and blot the spot until the food is gone.

Whether or not you like being the center of attention, sometimes it's unavoidable. Here's what to do when you find yourself center stage and speechless.

YOU DROP YOUR LUNCH TRAY IN FRONT OF THE WHOLE CAFETERIA

Whoops! You don't know *how* it happened, but with a loud crash you now find yourself standing in a pile of fish sticks and lime Jell-O cubes. Hang on a sec! Don't crawl under the nearest table. Try doing this instead:

Crack a joke. It's always better to have people laughing *with* you instead of *at* you.

YOU HAVE TO BE EXCEPTIONALLY GIFTED TO CREATE A MESS LIKE THIS!

Clean up the mess. Don't act so cool that you turn down offers from people who want to help. The sooner the mess is cleaned up, the sooner you're out of the spotlight. Pick up what you can and put it back on your tray. Let someone who works in the cafeteria know you spilled so they can mop up any slippery, slimy messes. If there's broken glass, don't touch anything—get an adult's help instead.

Clean up yourself. Even though you're now officially starving, it's better to deal with spills on your clothes sooner than later. The longer the food has to soak into the fibers, the harder it is to get out.

SURVIVAL SECRET

In a couple of hours—okay, maybe a day or so—no one will remember your accident but you. So let it go!

EW! Is that gum in your hair? Here's what to do when the gooey stuff gets you!

CLEANING UP GUM

PROBLEM	SOLUTION
GUM! In Your Hair	You'll need cold cream or peanut butter. Use three fingers (or a spoon) to scoop out a blob. Massage the blob into the gum. Keep doing this until the gum is loosened, then slide the blob—and the gum—down and out of your hair.
GUM! On Your Shoe	Hold an ice cube on the gum until it's frozen, then use a spoon to break off the brittle blob. Or, if there's no ice cube handy, scrape your shoe like crazy against the cement sidewalk, rubbing back and forth vigorously. A lamppost will do, too.
GUM! On the Carpet	Put a few ice cubes in a plastic bag. Hold the bag on the gum until it's frozen and brittle. Use a spoon to scrape off the gum.

YOUR PARENT LOSES A JOB

Losing a job is tough on a parent. It may make them feel sad or cranky or even nervous—especially about money. It also might mean you have to make some changes, like moving or not taking a planned family vacation. You may get teased at school, too. Other kids might ask you why your mom or dad doesn't have a job.

As hard as this may be for you, remember it's hard on your parent, too. And just like your parents are there for you in a pinch, it's your turn to pitch in and do what you can to make them feel better. Bring them breakfast in bed, take out the trash without having to be told, or ask what you can do to help. Try not to ask for things you know are expensive. But most importantly, tell them you love them.

SURVIVAL SECRET

Talk to your family about the situation and how you're feeling—especially if it's making you feel nervous and upset, too.

A FRIEND ASKS YOU TO STEAL

Even though you never want to let a friend down, sometimes you have to, if what they're asking you to do is wrong. Follow these strategies for standing strong.

It's your decision. Your friend can't *make* you do something you know is wrong. You're responsible for your own decisions and actions. Remember, if you get caught, you're the one who gets in trouble, not your friend.

Say no. Simply tell your friend you don't want to.

Stand firm. Your friend may tease and taunt you, even threaten not to be your friend or accuse you of not being a friend. This is the tough part. Focus on your *own* feelings about what you think is right and wrong.

Listen to that little voice inside your head that keeps reminding you that you are doing the right thing! Be confident that you are. Now…

HANG IN THERE, KID!

Walk away (even if it's hard to do). And be proud of yourself. There's **no shame** in doing the **right thing**.

P.S. If your friend keeps pressuring you to steal, especially when you've said you don't want to, you might want to find a new friend.

SURVIVAL SECRET
If you stand up for what you believe in, you're likely to find other friends who think like you do.

Do you have what it takes to get to the head of the class? Read on for all the right answers to teachers, tests, homework and more!

YOU'RE STARTING THE FIRST DAY OF SOMETHING NEW: SCHOOL (OR CAMP)

Beginning something new—whether it be starting at a new school, going to camp, or your first soccer practice with a new team—is exciting, but can also be a bit scary. Try these tips for making your first day a little bit easier.

Check it out first. The first day won't feel quite as strange if you're a little more familiar with the place you'll be. So check it out ahead of time. (And hey—if you don't know where to go, asking for directions is a great way to meet someone new!)

Make a friend. All it takes is one pal to make you feel a lot less alone. Introduce yourself to the person sitting next to you in class or standing behind you in the lunch line. Start a conversation by asking questions, like what they think that pile of yuck in the cafeteria is supposed to be.

Who else is new? You're probably not the only one, so keep your eye out for other new kids. If there are a lot of newbies, your school or camp might even have a special orientation before the first day.

Familiar comfort. Think about what you know is waiting for you at home, whether it be your favorite snack, your dog, or a huggable family member or friend.

SURVIVAL SECRET
Keep reminding yourself that each day will get a little bit easier. Because it will!

YOUR TEACHER IS MEAN

— Mean Teacher Checklist —

Put a check next to each statement that describes your teacher.

☑ Assigns too much homework.

☑ Yells at class for no reason.

☑ Acts annoyed when asked questions.

☑ Picks on me in front of everyone.

☑ Gives really hard tests.

If you checked one or more, see the **BIG TRUTH!**

Big Truth...

Is your teacher really **mean**, or is it possible that there's a good reason for their behavior? Take an **honest** look at your **own actions** and ask yourself: Could your teacher be annoyed because you ask him to **repeat** things you would have heard if you'd been listening? Does your teacher really yell at the class for *no reason*? No matter how small, **something** usually prompts it. How's your **attitude**? Does your teacher pick on you because of the way you act? And do you really think your teacher gives **hard tests** and lots of **homework** because she's mean—or because she's trying to help you **learn**? If you've honestly looked at your own behavior (and that of your classmates) and still feel that your teacher is **unkind** or **unfair**, talk to a parent or a school counselor and let them help you resolve your teacher troubles.

SURVIVAL SECRET

Remember, your teacher is there to **help** you, not **scare** you, and most teachers **really care** about being good teachers. However, when you have a teacher who really doesn't like you, do what you can to figure out how to win that teacher over to your side!

WHOOPS! I FORGOT...

Have you ever forgotten to do your homework, or have so much to do you just don't think you can finish it all? If so, read on!

Whether you forgot to do it, didn't get to it, or simply left it at home, 'fess up and **tell the truth**. Teachers can usually tell when students are making up stories. Not only will it annoy your teacher if you fib, but you'll look silly, too. Talk to your teacher alone, either before class or after, and explain what happened. Let them know that you're sorry. The first time it happens or if it doesn't happen often, your teacher is likely to understand—especially if you're being truthful.

I don't get it!

Sometimes you'll get an assignment that seems impossible. Don't worry! There are plenty of places you can turn to for help. Ask a teacher, a parent, or a librarian to explain the directions to you. If you *always* find homework in a certain class troublesome, consider signing up for a tutor—just a session or two may get you on the right track!

TOO MUCH HOMEWORK TO DO...

Believe it or not (though it can sometimes seem hard to believe) teachers don't give homework as torture, but to help you learn. The trick to getting it all done is to **manage your time wisely**. Try these tips for tackling your load.

Start at the Top

Make a list of all your assignments, starting with the ones that are due first and finishing with the ones that are due last. Now start at the top and work down.

Hardest First

Tackle the tough stuff while your mind is still fresh at the beginning of your homework routine. Save the easier assignments for later.

Baby Bites

Break up big assignments into bite-size portions. Look at your calendar and work back from the due date. Figure out how much you have to do each day to be finished on time. Then do it!

Make the Most of Your Minutes

Do some homework while you're riding on the bus, waiting to be picked up from soccer, or sitting in the doctor's waiting room. When you add up the minutes, small chunks of time actually equal a pretty big chunk. If you used those little time bits of time wisely, you could probably get a lot of homework done, too.

REPORTS: GETTING STARTED

The **due date** is creeping closer, and you haven't even picked a topic! Try these tips for getting unstuck and getting started.

WRITE ABOUT A MEMORABLE MOMENT IN HISTORY

Assignment:

Write about a memorable moment in history.

Brainstorm

Make a list of topics that are interesting to you. Write down as many ideas as you can. Don't stop to judge whether an idea is good or bad, just write! To get started, jot down:

1. Your favorite things to do.

2. Places you'd like to see.

3. Things you'd like to learn about.

Pick a topic

Check your list for a topic that fits your teacher's requirements. It may not be obvious at first, but one of your ideas can probably be molded to fit the assignment.

1) Favorite Things to Do
Baseball, playing guitar, reading

2) Places I'd like to See
Yankee Stadium, the Rocky Mountains, Australia

3) Things I'd like to Learn about
Aligators, Eskimoes, World Records

MY TOPIC:
When Babe Ruth Broke the Home Run World Record

Research

Good places to find information include:

1. books

2. encyclopedias

3. magazines

4. newspaper archives

5. museums

6. interviews

7. Internet

8. your school or local library (Ask the librarian for help!)

Write away!

With your topic decided and your research complete, you're ready to start writing.

SURVIVAL SECRET

Choose a topic that's interesting to you. It will make the assignment much more enjoyable.

CLASS PRESENTATION JITTERS

Speaking in front of your class can be a nerve-racking experience. Pretend you're an actor and follow this script:

Step One: Prepare
Know your topic! The more comfortable you are with the information, the more confident you'll feel presenting it.

Step Two: Practice
Practice in front of a mirror, speak into a tape recorder, or just stand alone in your room.

Step Three: Dress rehearsal
Present your report to your family. It gives you a chance to practice with an audience, and they're sure to offer support and helpful hints.

Step Four: Show time! When the big moment arrives, feel confident that you're prepared. Before you begin, take a few deep breaths to calm yourself. If you need to, find a friend or two in the audience to focus on for moral support. You might be nervous in the beginning, but once you get going, you're likely to feel more comfortable.

YOU'RE STUCK ON A TEST

Next time your mind draws a big BLANK, try these tips for troubleshooting even the toughest tests!

PROBLEM	SOLUTION
Multiple choice	These can be *tricky* since the answers often sound similar. Read all your choices. **Start by eliminating the answers you know are wrong.** Once you've narrowed down your choices, do your best at making a good guess.
True or false?	Warning! **It's easy to be fooled by a sentence that is only partly true.** Take your time and read each question carefully *before* you answer. Watch out for words like "always" or "never." Since few things are "always" or "never," they can be clues that the answer is false.
Essay topic	Carefully read the assignment and look for key words that tell you what is wanted in your essay and <u>underline</u> them. **Jot down ideas at the side of the page.** Now take that information and do your best to address the topic. Remember, an essay doesn't have to be long to be good.
Drawing a blank	**Try to write something down.** Work out the first part of the math equation, or jot down any information that may relate to your essay topic. If you have made an effort to show your thinking process, you will usually get partial credit. Once you start writing, you'll probably jolt your memory back into gear, too.

SURVIVAL SECRET

Read the directions carefully before starting! Begin with the questions you **do** know the answers to. **Save** the questions you **don't** know the answers to until the end.

TIPS FOR TALKING TO TEACHERS

There's a **right** way to talk to a teacher and a **wrong** way. Try the following strategies for getting the results you want.

Mind your manners

Be polite and respectful. Remember, you're trying to have a conversation, not a confrontation.

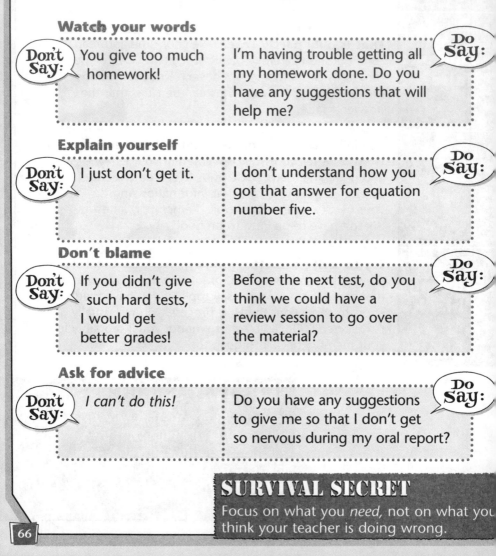

Watch your words

Don't Say: You give too much homework!

Do Say: I'm having trouble getting all my homework done. Do you have any suggestions that will help me?

Explain yourself

Don't Say: I just don't get it.

Do Say: I don't understand how you got that answer for equation number five.

Don't blame

Don't Say: If you didn't give such hard tests, I would get better grades!

Do Say: Before the next test, do you think we could have a review session to go over the material?

Ask for advice

Don't Say: I can't do this!

Do Say: Do you have any suggestions to give me so that I don't get so nervous during my oral report?

SURVIVAL SECRET

Focus on what you *need,* not on what you think your teacher is doing wrong.

YOU FIGHT WITH A FRIEND

Fighting with a friend is no fun! Don't let a silly fight turn into a big blow up, but if it does, try the following strategies for fixing your friendship.

1. **Act sooner than later.** The longer fights go unresolved, the angrier you'll feel. If your friend isn't ready to patch things up yet, don't push. Give him a few days to cool down and then try again.

2. **Make the first move.** Swallow your pride and do it! Someone has to, and it might as well be you (after all, you can control what you do, but not what your friend does).

3. **Talk calmly.** If the conversation gets heated, it's best to take a break and cool off.

4. **Hear each other out.** Let your friend state her case without interruptions. Ask your friend to do the same for you.

5. **Don't blame.** It will only put your friend on the defense. Instead, describe how your friend's actions made you *feel.*

6. **Fight fair.** There are some things that are so hurtful they should **never** be said! Also, don't bring up something that has *nothing* to do with what you're fighting about.

7. **Don't rattle off a list of everything wrong** your friend has ever done. Don't blame your friend for everything by saying things like "you never" or "you always". Stay focused on the current issue.

8. **Say** the magic words **"I'm sorry."** *Mean it*!

SURVIVAL SECRET

When talking it out, don't blame. Describe how your friend's actions make you *feel* instead. Say something like: "You really hurt my feelings when…"

WHEN YOUR FRIEND IS BETTER THAN YOU ARE (AT SCHOOL, IN SPORTS, OR WHATEVER)

Do you have a friend who *always* aces the weekly history quiz, even without studying? Does it make you wonder why you aren't as smart? Does it make you jealous or competitive? No matter who you are or what you're good at, the truth is that someone will **ALWAYS** be smarter than you or better at a sport, or whatever else you want to fill in the blank with! That's just life. And the quicker you come to accept it, the happier you'll be. But know this: feeling jealous or competitive is natural. Just don't get so overwhelmed by your feelings that it interferes with your friendship.

But guess what? Your friend may be naturally good at remembering dates and events, but have you noticed that *you're* BETTER at some other stuff? Like maybe you're a natural writer or great at making friends, or super at track and field.

So the next time you feel like your friend is outshining you, try this:

✔ *Think* about all the things *you're* good at.

✔ Try harder to get better at the things you're not as good at—*if you want to be better at them.*

✔ *Be proud of your friend* for having such superstar talents and be proud of yourself for being a good friend.

Now for the flip side: When you're better (faster, smarter) at something than your friend

Do you ever feel like your friend gets standoffish when you're always the one to win the game or get another A+ on your math test?

But, just like you can be jealous when someone else is better at something than you are, someone else is likely to be jealous of *you* for something you do better!

Here are some survival tips:

✔ Be happy for what you're good at.

✔ Don't be ashamed of your skills and talents if you're teased. But, at the same time, be sure you …

✔ Don't brag either.

✔ Accept that your friends might sometimes feel competitive. Friendly competition is okay.

From shared rooms to tattletales, getting along with siblings isn't always easy. Here's help for handling those sticky sibling situations!

POP QUIZ

When to tattle, when not to

Not all problems need a parent's help. But some do. Do you know the difference? Circle what you'd do in each situation.

1. You want to put on your favorite jeans and can't find them. Then you see them—wadded up in a ball on the floor of your sister's room. You...

   a. call your mom at work and insist she get mad at your sister right now.

   b. ask your sister to wash your jeans for you because you want to wear them—and tell her to ask before borrowing them next time.

2. You saw your brother smoking behind the gym at school. This isn't the first time it's happened. You...

   a. promise you won't tell if he makes your bed for a month.

   b. tell your parents what you saw.

3. You're playing basketball when your brother appears and grabs the ball away from you. You...

   a. call him a big meanie and run and tell your parents.

   b. try to work it out by suggesting he play ball with you.

4. Your sister is a straight-A student and you're not. She calls you stupid all the time, even though you've asked her to stop a million times. You...

   a. call her pizza face and tease her back.

   b. talk to your parents about the problem.

5. Every time it's your brother's turn to walk the dog, he threatens to give you a hard time if you don't do it for him. You...

   a. take your brother's turn walking the dog because you're afraid of what will happen if you don't.

   b. have a private conversation with your parents about the situation.

6. You're happily watching TV when your sister barges in and changes the channel. You...

   a. scream for Mom or Dad to come help you.

   b. make a deal with your sister that she can have control of the remote *when your show is over.*

To tell or not to tell?

Check your tattle total by giving yourself a point each time you circled **b.**

Tattletale! *(0-3 Points)*

You're too tempted to tattle! Don't rely on your parents to solve *all* your problems—especially the ones you can handle yourself. Ask yourself these questions first: Does the same problem keep happening even though you have tried to solve it before? Is your sibling doing something that could hurt themselves or someone else? If the answer is yes, talk to your parents. Otherwise, you should be able to handle it yourself.

Super Sibling *(4-6 Points)*

Smart sibling! You know the difference between what's serious and not so important. After all, why bother your parents with problems you can work out yourself? It's a wise sib who also knows when the situation is too serious to handle alone and when help from a parent is needed.

YOU HAVE TO SHARE YOUR ROOM

Sharing a bedroom with a sibling doesn't have to be painful if you take steps to make sure your shared space doesn't become a war zone!

1. Create your space. Use the furniture to divide the room. Agree that you can each set up your side any way you want.

2. Post it. Hang a bulletin board on each side of the room for displaying personal stuff, like photos, awards, and posters.

3. Keep clutter under wraps. Stash your stuff in a big basket with a lid, or in a laundry basket that you can slide under your bed.

4. Control the closet. Make sure that your clothes stay separate by tying a bandanna or scarf in the middle of the rod. Now keep to your sides!

5. Write room rules. Sit down and write a list of rules that you both agree on, such as quiet time for studying, lights out, and having friends in the room. Post the rules on your bulletin board. Also include times when you can each have the room to yourself.

① USE FURNITURE TO DIVIDE ROOM

② BULLETIN BOARDS ON EACH SIDE OF ROOM

③ BIG BASKETS WITH LIDS TO STASH STUFF

④ CLOSET WITH BANDANA IN MIDDLE OF ROD

⑤ ROOM RULE SHEET POSTED

HOUSE RULES

SURVIVAL SECRET

Make the most of a too-tight situation by treating your sibling's privacy and belongings the way you "hope" s/he'll treat yours.

YOU GET BLAMED FOR EVERYTHING

Do your parents expect more of you because you're older and "should know better"? It's nice to be given responsibility. Still, there's nothing more frustrating or unfair than being **wrongly accused**. You know you didn't do it! Now you have to convince your parents. So take a deep breath, be smart, and act—don't *re*act.

Try this:

1. Calmly tell your story.

2. Explain why it wasn't you who did what you were blamed for.

3. Say, "I'm telling you the truth."

And if they still don't believe you?

Unfortunately, you'll have to accept the consequences of your sibling's actions. It's unfair. You know you didn't do it, you were honest, that's all that you can do. Hopefully, the truth will come out, if not this time, then next, and your innocence will be proven!

IT'S NOT FAIR!

SURVIVAL SECRET

No matter what anyone thinks, you *know* you didn't do it. Focus on that instead of the unfairness of the situation.

WHEN YOU'RE TOO YOUNG TO DO WHAT YOU WANT

YOU'RE TOO YOUNG TO GO TO AN R-RATED MOVIE

YOU'RE TOO YOUNG TO SWIM WITHOUT ADULT SUPERVISION

YOU'RE TOO YOUNG TO STAY HOME ALONE WHILE WE'RE OUT OF TOWN

Who likes to hear that they're too young to do something or too young to understand something? No one, that's who! Not being included in a conversation or an activity because of your age can seem really unfair. Remember that whoever is excluding you probably isn't doing it to be mean, but to protect you (even if you don't think you need protecting). So trust their judgment, and be confident that...

You won't be too young for too long!

Everyone goes through hard times—a best friend moves away, your pet dies, or your grandma is really sick. Sometimes it feels like things will never get better, but there are ways to make it through—even when you think you won't.

YOUR PET DIES

Pets can be special friends, and just because they don't speak doesn't mean you don't think of your pet as a family member or good friend. So, when you lose a pet, it really hurts. Here are some things you can do to help with the healing process.

Give yourself permission to be sad and upset. It's normal and will help you heal. There's no right or wrong way to grieve, or even a special amount of time. Grieving is a personal process, to do in your own way.

Do what you can to express your feelings. Try writing in a journal, talking with a parent or friend, or having a good long cry.

Remember your pet. Save some of his belongings, like a food bowl, collar, or favorite toy in a box.

Have a service. This allows you to formally say goodbye and to share your feelings with others who loved your pet, too.

Think about the good times you had with your pet, and let yourself smile about them.

SURVIVAL SECRET

Before getting a new pet, understand that it's just that—new. It won't be a replacement for your old pet, but a completely different relationship (which promises to be wonderful, too).

SOMEONE YOU LOVE A LOT IS SICK

When someone close to you gets sick, it's scary. All of a sudden life feels very different—full of worry and anxiety and questions. Will the person get better? How long will it take? What if they die? Talk to your parents, a counselor, or friends about your feelings. Keeping these things bottled up inside won't make you feel better—just alone. **Ask questions.** Understanding the illness can help you be prepared for the outcome. Reach out to those who care about you and let them know what you're going through. Their support will help you. **Do things that make you feel happy**, like taking a bike ride, or making chocolate chip cookies. When visiting the sick person, try to be strong and positive, and let them know how much you love them. Comfort them by sharing stories about your life, or reading them your favorite book. But most of all, just being there is sure to brighten their day. Remember, they probably feel scared, too.

SURVIVAL SECRET
It's important to let the worry out somehow. If you're not comfortable talking about your feelings, write your thoughts down in a journal.

YOU MOVE AWAY FROM FRIENDS

Your parents just told you that in a few months, you'll be moving away. How can that be? Your friends are here, your school is here…your LIFE is here. And what's more: You don't know anyone *anywhere* else! So what do you do now? Well, you *could* try to talk your parents out of moving. But that probably wouldn't get you very far (they've probably already given it a lot of thought, and if you didn't have to move, you probably wouldn't be)! So what do you do next? You **take a deep breath** and begin to think about all the potentially *good* possibilities of moving (you've probably already dwelled on all the negative ones, so you don't need our help there!).

1. First off, know that wherever you're going, **you can ALWAYS stay in touch**. From e-mail to instant messaging to phoning, or even good old snail mail, there are plenty of ways to keep in touch.

   ✔ **Plan a weekly time to chat with a good friend.** (Check with your parents and agree on a time limit, first. Also, take turns calling so one person doesn't always get stuck with the bill.) You can also set up a group e-mail list so that you can keep in touch with all your friends at once.

   ✔ **Record a tape and mail it.** Tell a couple of jokes and share your new-place news.

   ✔ **Send a video or e-mail snapshots** of your new life so you can show your friends what your new neighborhood, school, and room are like.

2. Make a list of all the **great things** you have to look forward to, like:

✔ **New friends:** You'll have a whole new group to get to know (even if you're thinking: I'll never have any friends like the ones I have now: but you will). It may take a while to feel as happy with your new friends as you do with your old ones, but it WILL happen. And the best thing about new friends is that they won't remember any of the embarrassing moments that your old friends tease you about! You're starting with a clean slate!

✔ **New activities:** Most likely, your new neighborhood will have a soccer team, karate class, or swimming pool for you to keep on doing the things you love to do. But moving to a new place also lets you try out new activities. It's also a great way to meet a bunch of new friends who are interested in the same things you are!

✔ **New sights to see:** When you first move, you can pretend you're on vacation because you're in a new place and play tourist. Go on a walk through your neighborhood and take a camera so that you can record all the new sights.

> ## SURVIVAL SECRET
>
> Just because you've moved away, doesn't mean you can't still be best friends. You just might discover a whole new side of your friend by keeping in touch long-distance.

✔ **New news to report back:** Just as when you come back from vacation and have a lot to share with your friends, same thing with moving away. Your old friends will want to hear from you (and hear what you're up to): you're the one, after all, with the exciting new life!

NOW Test Your Survival Skills!

You've done it! From bee stings to broken bones, bullies to bloody noses, now that you've read this book, you can officially say you've learned how to survive all sorts of situations! You've also learned some important **strategies** that can be used to solve any problem. Take this final quiz, then check your score to find out your survival know-how now. How much have you learned since the quiz you took at the beginning of the book?

1. You're lying in the tub, talking on the phone, when a **thunderstorm** comes rolling in. You glance out the window and keep chatting with your pal.

    a. That's me
    b. I might do that
    c. I'd never do that

2. You're on a hike with some friends when you realize **you're lost**! You immediately split up in different directions and go look for the way out.

    a. That's me
    b. I might do that
    c. I'd never do that

3. You're at the zoo talking to someone nice who says she's the zookeeper's assistant. You didn't see her earlier and **you're not sure who she is**. But she says the zookeeper has some lion photos she thinks you'd like to see. You hesitate, but then write down your e-mail address and give it to her anyway.

    a. That's me
    b. I might do that
    c. I'd never do that

4. You're on a hike and your group is **running low on water**. You decide to keep going and get to the top of the mountain anyway, even though it's 3 miles away.

    a. That's me
    b. I might do that
    c. I'd never do that

5. You're visiting your grandparent's farm and you think you see a **snake hiding under the porch** steps. You immediately get a stick and start poking at it so it'll come out and you can get a better look.

   a. That's me
   b. I might do that
   c. I'd never do that

6. You're **skateboarding down the sidewalk** when a pedestrian steps in your way. You say "excuse me" and pass on their right.

   a. That's me
   b. I might do that
   c. I'd never do that

Check Your Survival Skills!

Give yourself two points for every **c** you circled and one point for every **b**. Give yourself zero points for every **a**.

Super Survivor (9-12 points)

You're ready to tackle just about anything! Keep using your head. Your good sense and smart thinking will get you out of all sorts of sticky situations.

Satisfactory Survivor (5-8 points)

There's still room for improvement. Keep this book handy and check out the last page of this guide.

SOS–Save Our Survivor! (0-4 points)

Another read through this guide is probably a good idea!

HOW TO SURVIVE JUST ABOUT ANYTHING ELSE

Armed with *How to Survive Almost Anything*, you should feel prepared to handle and survive just about any situation. So **now it's time to go and face whatever life throws your way.** You've learned how to handle a lot of things from reading this book. But how about everything else? Here are some strategies that can be helpful to you no matter what situation you find yourself in:

✔ **Stay calm** (in an emergency). You'll be better able to focus and figure out what to do.

✔ **Be polite.** It's amazing how far a simple "please," "thank you," or "I'm sorry" will take you.

✔ **Right wrongs.** That means admitting you're wrong when you are and saying you're sorry.

✔ Don't automatically trust adults just because they're adults. **Adults aren't always right or trustworthy.**

✔ If you're **uncomfortable** doing something, **don't do it**! (It doesn't matter if everyone else is doing it.) Standing up to peer pressure isn't easy. But it can be harder to do something (and live with it afterward) that you know you probably shouldn't have done.

✔ **Don't take yourself so seriously.** (If you can make light of your embarrassments, others will be able to go easy on you too!)

✔ **Share** what you're feeling with others (and how they make you feel). Don't assume they'll know what's going on with you otherwise.

✔ **Be good to yourself.** You'll feel your best if you get the right balance of sleep, food, and fun!